William Canby Biddle

William Canby of Brandywine, Delaware

His descendants fourth to seventh generation in America

William Canby Biddle

William Canby of Brandywine, Delaware
His descendants fourth to seventh generation in America

ISBN/EAN: 9783337329549

Printed in Europe, USA, Canada, Australia, Japan

Cover: Foto ©ninafisch / pixelio.de

More available books at **www.hansebooks.com**

WILLIAM CANBY,

OF

BRANDYWINE, DELAWARE.

" Mark the perfect man, and behold the upright, for the end of that man is peace."

HIS DESCENDANTS

FOURTH TO SEVENTH GENERATION

IN AMERICA.

PRINTED FOR PRIVATE DISTRIBUTION,
PHILADELPHIA,
— 1883.

IN MEMORY OF

WILLIAM AND MARTHA CANBY.

William Canby, grandson of Thomas Canby who came to America in 1683, was the son of Oliver Canby, who married Elizabeth Shipley in the year 1744 and settled at Brandywine, where his son William resided from his birth in 1748, until his death in 1830.

He married Martha Marriott, of Bristol, Pa., who was born at Trenton in 1747, and died in 1826. She was the daughter of Thomas Marriott, the son of Thomas, and grandson of Isaac Marriott, who came to this country and settled in New Jersey in 1680.

After the marriage of William and Martha Canby in 1774, their humble but pleasant and comfortable home was a small two-story brick house, containing, on the ground floor, only a "living-room" and kitchen.

To this was attached a frame building, consisting of an out-kitchen and wood-house below, with two sleeping-rooms above.

The dwelling faced with a fair frontage toward the Brandywine, but the depth sufficed for a single room only; the living-
room was a cheerful apartment, with an old-fashioned corner
chimney, where a bright wood-fire burned in a Franklin stove;
this was finally replaced by a grate for anthracite coal, one of
the first two used in Wilmington.

On a corner of the mantel piece above it lay the New Tes-
tament, the life of Lady Guion, and Pope's Essay on Man.
William Canby's usual seat was on a chair beside the fire-place,
and from the volumes named he read daily for several hours;
although reading for himself, he preferred to read aloud but in
a low tone, so as not to disturb those around him.

A volume of history, the journal of John Woolman, Thos.
Ellwood, or some other "ancient worthy," was sometimes
substituted for the life of Lady Guion, but he rarely read from
the writings of any poet except Pope, although he frequently
repeated Montgomery's beautiful lines on Prayer, also those
beginning "Spirit leave thine house of clay," and Pope's Uni-
versal Prayer.

On the southerly side of the "living-room," a window and
glass door looked out on the large old-fashioned garden, which
was bright with flowers all through the season, and also sup-
plied the small fruits and vegetables for family use.

There was a yard in front and at the side, in which stood
a fine locust tree and three weeping willows that shaded the
house and gave it a pleasant rural appearance.

The new part at the westerly end, consisting of a parlor and entry, was added in 1809.

The building still stands at the corner of Sixteenth and King Streets, but is much changed in appearance and character; the grassy yard is gone, the old part of the house, which contained the "living-room" and kitchen, is divided into two small tenant houses, the new part has been enlarged by the addition of a front porch, third story and back buildings, so that it presents a comfortable appearance.

Humble as this home was, it held a very happy family; no pictures hung upon its walls, no ornaments except natural flowers were there, but it was adorned in its severe simplicity and plainness by the presence of parents, who, in obedience to that Indwelling Light which they publicly professed to follow, were found prompt to evidence their religion, pure and undefiled before their God and Father, by their readiness "to visit the fatherless and widows in their affliction, and to keep unspotted from the world."

The influence of their Christian graces, their gentleness and truth united the household in the bonds of love and peace; cheerful social intercourse brightened its atmosphere, and a sincere unostentatious hospitality welcomed the frequent guest to its customary simple fare.

This was rendered possible only by the admirable management, thrift and energy of the excellent help-meet of William Canby.

Eminently gifted as he was with ability to lay up treasures where " neither moth nor rust doth consume," he was utterly lacking in the worldly talent of adding houses to lands, but the narrow means of the household, under the able administration of its maternal head, sufficed to meet the outlay for all actual necessities, although nothing was left to expend upon superfluities or for indulgence in useless luxuries.

Restricted means enforced close economy, the housework was mainly performed by the members of the family, but this never interfered with the openhearted reception of all who could properly claim a welcome at this cheerful Christian home.

Truly independent in the possession of a small income, from means which would not now suffice for the annual disbursements of a liberal household, but which to them, with their modest wants, proved a competency, here William and Martha Canby educated and brought up a family of children, who, in their various allotments in life, never forgot the loving lessons of their youth, and seldom neglected the performance of any duty required at their hands.

The difficulties of a narrow income were thoroughly experienced by them to their lasting advantage, but the example always before them of the denial of self for the benefit of others, so beautifully moulded their characters, that sympathizing kindness was their rule of action, and when in after years ability was afforded, the open hand ever responded to the dictates of the loving heart.

The oldest son, Oliver, led a very quiet and secluded life, being generally employed upon a farm ; he died at the advanced age of 83 years.

The youngest child was named Marriott ; he was, however, generally called Merrit, and his father had such an objection to the designation of persons by any other than their correct names, that he changed his son's to that usually given to him.

Inheriting from his mother a resolute and energetic spirit, Merrit Canby left home early to obtain a mercantile education in Philadelphia. About the year 1830 he associated with himself as a partner Joseph S. Lovering, who was the first to successfully introduce into the United States the improved process of boiling sugar by steam in vacuum.

This connexion proved mutually advantageous, and Merrit Canby retired from business in the latter part of the year 1835. His local and family attachments then drew him back to Wilmington, the strong ties of kindred and old acquaintance never having been weakened by absence. Here he lived during the remainder of his long life, actively engaged in furthering the philanthropic and public interests of his native place.

An attractive sweetness and gentleness characterized the sisters ; various as were their temperaments, few women have had more warmly attached friends or have left records of greater simplicity and purity of life than Fanny Ferris, Mary Biddle and Anna C. Smyth ; the ancestral name does not descend through them, but may their children and children's children to the latest generation never prove unworthy of it.

Any description of the household of William and Martha Canby would be very incomplete, which did not mention their adopted children Hannah and Mary Gibbons; they were the daughters of William Canby's sister, Mary, who married Abraham Gibbons of Lampeter, Penna.

He died of yellow fever in 1798, after attending the Yearly Meeting held in Philadelphia in the autumn of that year; his wife had died in the previous year; upon his decease his daughters, aged three and five years respectively, were brought to Brandywine, and from that time made part of the family there.

No parental kindness could have watched over children with more faithful and loving care than these orphans received in their adopted home, and none could have repaid this care with truer filial devotion.

When the older members of the family left the protecting roof of their childhood for homes of their own, these nieces remained to discharge all the offices of love, by watching over the declining years and ministering to the infirmities of their aged adopted parents with patient devotion to the close of their lives.

After the death of William Canby, Hannah and Mary Gibbons continued to live in the old homestead for five years, when the marriage of the elder sister to a member of the family removed them to another home, where the tie of kindred was perpetuated during the remainder of their lives.

William Canby, his brother Samuel and his half-brother William Poole, resided near each other, and their three families were in the habit of familiar and affectionate daily intercourse.

The following account of William Canby is extracted from the note book of his son-in-law, Benjamin Ferris:

"William Canby, son of Oliver Canby and Elizabeth Shipley, married Martha Marriott, daughter of Thomas Marriott and Sarah Smith, of Bristol, Penna., 5th month 5th, 1774.

"They settled in Wilmington, on the south side of Brandywine, (in a brick building erected originally for the kitchen part of a larger establishment) in the summer of 1774. Here they lived (excepting one short period) until the year 1809, when a larger building was added to it, making a much more commodious residence. In this house William Canby and his wife lived together, enjoying the blessings of peace and quiet, about seventeen years, surrounded by dutiful and affectionate children, and having a sufficiency to supply the moderate desires of minds like theirs, governed by a just estimate of the things of time. This happy connection was at length dissolved by the decease of Martha Canby on the 18th day of the Eighth month, 1826. To the affectionate heart of William Canby this was a severe stroke, but he bore it, as he had always borne the dispensations of Divine Providence, with that composure and equanimity which comport with the character of a Christian. He passed the remainder of his life in meek and humble submission to the Divine Will, and after a separation from the object of his youthful attachment of about three years and eight months, he quietly departed this life, the third day of the Fourth month, 1830, in the eighty-second year of his age.

"In early life he received, by a fall, an injury to the head, from the effects of which he never was wholly relieved. For many years during the middle part of his life he had periodical headaches of the most distressing character, so heavy as to produce what he used to term "lethargy;" under this suffering, he resorted to the use of steam-baths, by which he mostly obtained great relief. Though endowed by nature with vigorous . intellectual powers, and fitted by education for carrying on business, he was obliged to relinquish a lucrative concern in the bright meridian of life, and to retire from business upon a very limited income; but in humble acquiescence to the will of Him in whom he trusted, *that* little, like the widow's cruise, "failed not." With the aid of a most faithful and efficient partner and companion, he not only brought up five children to be useful, respectable members of the community, but was himself an active and untiring benefactor to the poor. To those in affliction and to him that had no helper, William Canby was ever ready to administer both by his personal attentions and by his sympathy; and such was his benevolence, that he often denied himself the common comforts of life, that he might assist those who were in distress. I have known him frequently, in bitter cold weather, to go and stop a hole in some poor man's cabin, or to mend his roof that he might be sheltered from the rain, and when the means in his power did not suffice to meet all the cases of suffering around him, he used exertions to enlist others in the service.

"His person was slender; his height rather below middle size, about 5 feet 6 inches; he was very temperate in diet, using the simplest food in a very moderate quantity. Though slender in person his limbs were muscular, and he was not only fond of action but used a great deal of it, frequently walking five, six or seven miles from home to visit a neighboring meeting, or to brighten the chain which bound him to his friend or relatives living at a distance. To the latest period of life he retained a large portion of his natural activity both of body and mind, for there was nothing sluggish in either. His temper was quick and his feelings acute, they very seldom were suffered to betray him into any unguarded expressions, but whenever he apprehended that anything had escaped him calculated to wound another, he never felt satisfied until he had gone to the person and made acknowledgment of his offence; and such was his tenderness on this point, that he often found, after making his apologies, that no wound had been inflicted. He was truly an humble Christian, following in the footsteps of the pure and holy Pattern with faithfulness, and attaining the object in a degree seldom experienced. Never have I known a man of more pure disinterestedness of character, nor one in whom the selfish principles of our nature seemed to be more perfectly subjected to the Divine Power of Goodness, which dictated the precept "Thou shalt love thy neighbor as thyself."

Veiled under the garment of humility and making no display, the natural powers of his mind were of a very high order He had considerable knowledge of practical mathematics, a profound insight into the nature of the solar system, and much solid information in the departments of history, biography and natural science." B. F.

The following lines, hastily written and not corrected, were found among the papers of a grandchild who died in 1833; no other death has occurred among the eighteen grandchildren in the intervening fifty years.

"On reading in Niles' weekly Register an editorial notice of the death of William Canby.

"Why should the stranger pen the line,
    The tribute to thy virtues bright?
Or offer on devotion's shrine,
    The incense to religion's might?

"Were we in dedication's path,
    To follow humbly where thou trod;
In Christian meekness while on earth,
    And holy confidence in God.

"Then would thy virtues brighter shine,
    In hearts that claim a kindred tone;
Nor should the stranger pen the line,
    Thy monument of worth alone.

"The lives of thy frail children here,
    A lasting tribute to thy praise,
Through time a monument would rear,
.   That pointing heavenward would raise.
Bright tokens that would ever shine
    As gems upon thy diadem,
Eternal and divine.

"As stars upon thy crown of light,
    Rejoicing evermore ;
    These children of immortal life,
    Thy monument of power."

                                        M. B.

The editorial referred to, appeared in Niles' Register, published at Baltimore, 5th month 8th, 1830.

As that paper was devoted to politics and statistics, and
rarely if ever admitted obituaries, the notice of Wm. Canby's
death occasioned some surprise. It read as follows :

"William Canby, an aged and much beloved member of
the Society of Friends, died at Wilmington, Delaware, and his
remains were interred on the 4th ult.

"If it were possible to suppose that any one man was less
offensive than any of the rest of his kind, more separated from
worldly affairs, more willing to perform deeds of charity and
benevolence, less guilty of a bad thought or capable of a bad
action, we should have fixed upon William Canby as being
that man.

"He was the author of a letter to Mr. Jefferson, in 1813,
which, with the reply, was very extensively published.

"While the body of the deceased good man was suspended

over the grave that had been made to receive it (as is the custom of Friends at the interment of aged and valued members), a deep silence prevailed for a short time, as though the numerous assembly had even ceased to breathe.   It was interrupted by a clear and solemn female voice saying, This is not death but life everlasting.

"The body was then deposited in the earth, and the company left the burying ground as though just separated from an immortal spirit."

The letter was as follows :

Wilmington, 8th month 29th, 1813.
" Esteemed friend Thomas Jefferson,

I have for years felt at times affection towards thee, with a wish for thy salvation ; to wit, the attainment, while on this stage of time in the natural body, of a suitable portion of *divine life ;* for, otherwise, we know little more than the life of nature, and therein are in danger of becoming inferior to the beasts which perish, in consequence of declining the offers of divine life made to every rational being.

"I have long had better hopes of thee (particularly in our little quiet meeting yesterday) that thou hast been faithful, at least over a few things, and I wish thou mayest become ruler over more, and enter into the joy of our Lord and into his rest ; and it occurred to me, in order thereto, that we should become Christians, for he that hath not the spirit of Christ is none of His, and this knowledge and belief are, I think, strongly in-

sisted on by divers of the Apostles, who had personally seen
and were eye-witnesses to his majesty, particularly in the
Mount, and by others who had not that in view; which, however, was insufficient to perfect them and was to be taken away,
that they might be more effectually turned to that Spirit, which
leadeth into all truth, whose power alone is able to reduce the
spirits of nature to suitable silence and submission.

Thy friend,

(Signed) William Canby."

Reply by Thomas Jefferson :

" Sir !

I have duly received your favor of August 29th,
and am sensible of the kind intentions from which it flows, and
truly thankful for them ; the more so, as they could only be the
result of a favorable estimate of my public course, as much devoted to study as a faithful transaction of the trust committed
to me would permit.

" No subject has occupied more of my consideration, than
our relations with all the beings around us, our duties to them
and our future prospects.

" After bearing all which can probably be suggested con-
cerning them, I have formed the best judgement I could, as to
the course they prescribe, and in the due observance of that
course, I have no reflections which give me uneasiness.

" An eloquent preacher of your religious society, Richard
Mott, in a discourse of much unction and pathos, is said to have

exclaimed aloud to his congregation that "he did not believe
there was a Quaker, Presbyterian, Methodist or Baptist in
Heaven."

"Having paused to give his congregation time to stare and
wonder, he added "in Heaven God knows no distinction, but
considers all good men as his children and brethren of the same
family."

"I believe with the Quaker preacher, that he, who observes
those moral precepts in which all religions concur, will never be
questioned at the gates of Heaven, as to the dogmas in which
all differ; that on entering there, all these are left behind, and
that the Aristides and Catos, the Penns and Tillotsons, Presby-
terians and Papists will find themselves united in all the principles which are in concert with the Supreme Mind.

"Of all the systems of morality, ancient or modern, which
have come under my observation, none appears so pure as that
of Jesus.

"He who follows this steadily need not, I think, be uneasy,
although he cannot comprehend the subtilties and mysteries
erected on the doctrines of Jesus by those who, calling themselves his special followers and favorites, would make him come
into the world to lay snares for all understandings but *theirs*.

"Their metaphysical heads, usurping the judgment seat of
God, denounce as *his* enemies all who cannot perceive the logic
of Euclid, in the demonstrations of St. Athanasius that three
are one, and one, three.

"In all essential points you and I are of the same religion, and I am too old to go into the unessentials.

"Repeating, therefore, my thankfulness for the kind concern you have been so good as to express, I salute you with friendship and brotherly love.

(Signed)　　THOMAS JEFFERSON."

Monticello, Sept. 18th, 1813.

Martha Marriott (wife of Wm. Canby) was the great granddaughter of Isaac Marriott, who emigrated to America in 1680.

Thomas Marriott (son of Isaac) married Martha Kirkbride; their son, Thomas Marriott, born the 21st day of the 12th month (called February) 1717–18, O.S., married, on the 20th day of 7th month (September), 1739, Shobal and Prudence Smith's daughter—Sarah—who was born the 2nd day of 9th month (November) 1720, O.S. Their daughter Martha was born at Trenton, N. J., 7th month, 25th, 1747.

Sarah Marriott's older sister, Mary, married Thos. Shipley, settled in Ridley, and removed to Brandywine in 1755; through her and her daughters, the Canbys are related to the Shipleys, Buckleys and Newlins.

Martha Canby was a woman of superior character, thoroughly sympathizing with her husband in his obedience to the command, "Seek ye first the kingdom of God and his righteousness;" she trusted, as regards the needs of this life, that "all these things shall be added" to those who properly avail themselves of the talents committed to their keeping, and feel the force of the injunction, "provide things honest in the sight of all men."

With ability which would have fitted her to administer liberal things with a liberal hand, she accepted the privations incident to small means with the greatest cheerfulness and sweetness, thereby evincing the real strength of her character and effectually ministering to the comfort of her household.

The following notice, by B. Ferris, appeared shortly after her decease, which occurred 8th month 18th, 1826 :—

"Died, on the 18th inst., in this borough, aged nearly 79 years, Martha, wife of William Canby.

"Although the deceased 'went to her grave in full age, like as a shock of corn cometh in in his season,' yet she did not outlive the period of her usefulness.

"By her husband and children she was respected and venerated, both for the purity and excellence of her character, and as the efficient head of the domestic department. With a mind of more than common vigor, she remained the watchful guardian of her family, and had, until her last illness, the pleasure of being actively engaged in promoting their welfare.

"Her death, therefore, is felt, not like the fall of a supernumerary, but as the removal of a pillar out of its place, leaving her survivors to mourn the loss of an affectionate relative and friend, and to feel, with increasing pressure, the trials common to us all, in this probationary state.

" As a christian, her example was worthy of all commenda-
tion, for although she never obtruded herself on public attention
by the loudness of her profession, she was very careful to obey
the injunctions of "pure and undefiled religion." Unlike the
one who said "I go" and went not, her life was a standing
testimony to the superior excellence of *practical* christianity;
and now if an unspotted youth, a faithful attention for fifty-two
years to the various duties of a wife, a mother and a friend, if
beneficence to the poor, sympathy with the afflicted and
benevolence to all, may afford survivors a well grounded hope
for the deceased, then may we rest in the happy assurance that
she has been taken from the field of useful labor to receive the
plaudit, ' Well done good and faithful servant.' "

Such were the sterling characteristics of our ancestors
William and Martha Canby.

In the note book of Benjamin Ferris, from which most of
this memoir has been extracted, after an account of his (Ferris)
progenitors, he addresses his children thus, " No immoral, no
intemperate, no vicious person is to be found, from the remotest
time down to the present, in the line of our ancestors (Ferris)
on either the male or female side of the house.

"The same may be said in relation to the ancestry of my
children, on their mother's side (Canby); no family, perhaps,
can point to a more pure original.

"Honest, industrious, conscientious, and for all these excellent qualities standing conspicuous, my children have, in

their ancestry, all that a noble and excellent example can give
to encourage them to emulate such worthy patterns ; where
much is given, much is rationally required.

" Let those who follow in the line of such excellent ancestors
beware that they cast no stain or spot on the family, lest one
should stand out in bold relief as first man or woman for more
than 180 years, whose conduct is calculated to raise a blush, or
wound the feelings of those who value their family, not for its
honors, not for its titles, not for its wealth, but for its virtues.
B.F. 2d month 5th, 1838."

The descendants of William Canby, following the common
lot of humanity, have encountered widely varied fortune in the
prosecution of their secular pursuits.

Trial, privation, wealth, ease, struggle and abundance have
been theirs; adversity and prosperity have been meeted out,
to some the one, to some the other, but they have verified the
truth of the old saying :—

"I have been young and now am old, yet have I not seen
the righteous forsaken nor his seed begging bread."

CANBY FAMILY IN ENGLAND.

BENJAMIN CANBY,

OF

THORN, YORKSHIRE.

IN AMERICA.

FIRST AND SECOND GENERATION.

Benjamin Canby, England,

to

William Canby, Brandywine, Delaware.

Benjamin Canby, of Thorn, in Yorkshire, England, had three children, Benjamin, Thomas and Mary.

Thomas, when about 16 years old, emigrated to this country with his maternal uncle, Henry Baker, who, probably, paid his passage, and in return claimed his services as a laborer on his farm.

In an old account book, called "Registry of Arrivals," one finds

"in Capt. Jefferies shipp"

"Henry Baker, from Walton, in Lancashire, and Margaret, his wife, and their daughters Rachel, Rebecca, Phebe and Hester, and Nathan and Samuel, their sons; Mary Berkert, and ten other servants, named John Siddell, for 4 years, Henry Siddell, 4 years, James Yates, 5 years, Thomas Canby, Joseph Pferror, 4 years, Deborah Booth, 4 years, and others, all except Thomas Canby having their term of service named.

Thomas Canby, not being satisfied, appealed to Friends, and the Quarterly Meeting of Bucks County effected an amicable arrangement, as the minutes of that meeting yet show. After he arrived at man's estate, he purchased valuable lands in that county; he was enterprising and successful, and left a large number of lineal descendants.

His first wife was Sarah Jerves, whom he married 9th month, 2nd, 1693. She died 2nd month, 3rd, 1708, leaving eight children, two sons, Thomas and Benjamin (second), and six daughters. The married names of the latter were Sarah Hill, Elizabeth Lacy, Mary Hamton, Phebe Smith, Esther White and Martha Gillingham. They and their brothers all had many children.

Thomas Canby married 4th of 2nd month, 1709, Mary, daughter of Evan and Jean Oliver; by this second marriage he had eight children, viz.: Jane Paxson, Rebekah Wilson, Hannah, Joseph, Rachel, Oliver (our ancestor), Ann; and Lydia Johnson.

Mary Canby died the 26th day of 3d month, 1721.

Thomas Canby married a third time, his last wife's maiden name being Preston.

Oliver Canby bore his mother's maiden name; he settled in Wilmington about 1740, where he owned the first mill built within the limits of the corporation; it stood about 200 yards above the present bridge.

He married 2nd month, 12th, 1744 O. S., or 4th month,

23rd, N. S., Elizabeth, daughter of William and Mary Shipley; their children were Hannah, William (our ancestor), Samuel, and Mary, who married Abraham Gibbons.

Oliver Canby died, after a sudden and severe illness, in his 38th year; he was in the prime of life, in the midst of a prosperous growing business, with an amiable wife, a young family, and every prospect that could gratify the desire of a reasonable man.

Mary Oliver was the fifth child of Evan and Jean Oliver, who emigrated from Radnorshire, Wales, "about ye beginning of ye 6 month, 1682, and arrived at Uplands (now Chester), in Pennsylvania, in America, ye 28th of ye 8 month, 1682." By this date it appears that Mary Oliver came over in the ship with William Penn.

Her birth is entered in an old "Oliver" account book: "The 5 was Marry the 9 day of the 10 month, 1677, the first day of the weeke." And her death thus: "Sister Mary Canby departed out of this world the 26 day of March, 1721; she was of the age of 43 years; a virtous [sic] woman."

The name Oliver, in the Wilson, Hamton, Paxson and Canby families, is derived from her.

Elizabeth Shipley, born in Leicester, England, in 1722, came with her parents to America when three years old. She married Oliver Canby in 1744, enjoying with him a happy union of about ten years; remaining his widow about seven years, she then married William Poole, whom she outlived about ten years, dying in 1789.

The following notice is from William Canby's Bible:

"Our dear mother, Elizabeth Poole, departed this life on First day morning, 11th month, 15th, 1789, in the sixty-seventh year of her age, in lamb-like quietude, having been of an innocent life and conversation, tenderly concerned for her children, and a good example of industry. That we may be enabled to follow her example in the gifts wherein the remembrance of her is precious, is my desire."

Her father, William Shipley, in 1736, built the house in Brandywine, which continued to be the property of his descendants until the present year [1883].

Like other old landmarks, it is about to yield to the destroying hand of improvement.

It was the largest dwelling house in the city. Friends' Meeting was held in it for two years before the first meeting house was erected.

GENEALOGY.

TYPE AND COLOR

Indicate Different Generations and Persons

Intermarried Therewith.

𝔉𝔦𝔯𝔰𝔱 𝔊𝔢𝔫𝔢𝔯𝔞𝔱𝔦𝔬𝔫—𝔙𝔦𝔬𝔩𝔢𝔱.

Second Generation—Red.

Third Generation—Black.

Fourth Generation—Green.

Fifth Generation—Violet.

Sixth Generation—Red.

Seventh Generation—Black.

GENEALOGY.

Thomas Canby;—B. 1667; came to America 1683, 16 years old; D. 9th month 20th, 1742, aged 75 years. M. first, Sarah Jerues, 9th month, 2nd, 1693; she died 2nd month 3rd, 1708. M. second, Mary Oliver, daughter of Evan and Jean Oliver, 2nd month 4th, 1709.

Mary Canby;—B. 10th month 9th, 1677, D. 1st month 26th, 1721, O. S.

SECOND GENERATION.

Thomas and Sarah Canby.

Benjamin, Sarah Hill, Elizabeth Lacy, Mary Hamton, Phebe Smith, Esther White, Thomas Benjamin, (second), and Martha Gillingham.

All of them, except the first Benjamin, left large families.

(31)

Thomas and Mary Canby.

Jane Paxson, Rebecca Wilson, Hannah, Joseph, Rachel, Oliver (our ancestors), Ann and Lydia Johnson.

Oliver Canby;—B. 3rd month 7th, 1717; D. 11th month 30th, 1754, aged 37 years, 8 months.

M. 4th month 23rd, 1744, N. S., Elizabeth, daughter of William and Mary Shipley.

THIRD GENERATION.

Oliver and Elizabeth Canby.

Canby, Hannah;—B. 1st month 2nd, 1746; D. 6th month 4th, 1748, N. S.

Canby, William;—B. 10th month 6th, 1748, N. S.; D. 4th month 3rd, 1830.

Canby, Samuel;—B. 8th month 6th, 1751; D. 3rd month 8th, 1832.

Canby, Mary;—B. 10th month 10th, 1754; D. 3rd month 26th, 1797.

Mary married *Abraham Gibbons.*

Canby, William;—B. 7th month 25th, or 10th month 6th, N. S., 1748; D. 4th month 3rd, 1830.

Married *Martha Marriott.*

Martha Canby;—B. 7th month 25th, or 10th month 6th, N. S., 1747; M. 5th month 5th, or 7th month 16th, N. S., 1774; D. 8th month 18th, 1826.

FOURTH GENERATION.

William and Martha Canby.

Canby, Oliver;—B. 3rd month 15th, 1775; D. 4th month 1st, 1858.

Canby, Sarah;—B. 11th month 1st, 1776; D. in infancy. . .

Canby, Fanny, wife of Benjamin Ferris. He was B. 8th month 7th, 1780; D. 11th month 9th, 1867.

Fanny Ferris;—B. 6th month 11th, 1778; M. 5th month 17th, 1804; D. 8th month 3rd, 1833.

Canby, Mary, wife of Clement Biddle. He was B. 8th month 10th, 1778; D. 2nd month 10th, 1856.

Mary Biddle;—B. 2nd month 11th, 1780; M. 11th month 2nd, 1810; D. 4th month 12th, 1849. . .

Canby, Sarah (second);—B. 7th month 12th, 1782; D. 3rd month 25th, 1783. . .

Canby, Anna, wife of David Smyth. He was B. 1st month 30th, 1783; D. 2nd month 5th, 1866.

    Anna C. Smyth;—B. 12th month 29th, 1784; M. 10th month 12th, 1815; D. 12th month 12th, 1867.

Canby, Marriott, changed to Merrit;—B. 10th month 9th, 1787; D. 12th month 10th, 1866.

    Married Eliza Tatnall Sipple.

    Eliza T. Canby;—B. 9th month 6th, 1795; M. 5th month 20th, 1830; D. 10th month 26th, 1865.

FIFTH GENERATION.

Fanny and Benjamin Ferris.

Ferris, William;—B. 2nd month 18th, 1805; D. 7th month 12th, 1805.

Ferris, Edward;—B. 7th month 24th, 1809; D. 8th month 31st, 1810.

Ferris, Anna;—B. 11th month 27th, 1811; D. 9th month 29th, 1814.

Ferris, Deborah;—B. 7th month 22nd, 1813.

Ferris, Anna M.;—B. 6th month 11th, 1815.

Ferris, Benjamin;—B. 4th month 2nd, 1817; D. 10th month 29th, 1831.

Ferris, Martha;—B. 6th month 25th, 1819.

Ferris, David;—B. 7th month 16th, 1821. Married Sarah Ann Underwood.

> Sarah Ann Ferris;—B. 8th month, 1828; M. 4th month 12th, 1849.

Ferris, William;—B. 12th month 14th, 1821. Married Mary Wetherald.

> Mary W. Ferris;—B. 12th month 22nd, 1825; M. 1st month 1st, 1845.

Ferris, Edward;—B. 12th month 20th, 1821. Married Catherine Lehman Ashmead.

> Catherine L. Ferris;—B. 7th month 1st, 1833; M. 6th month 5th, 1855.

Mary and Clement Biddle.

Biddle, Martha;—B. 10th month 21st, 1811; D. 1st month 25th, 1833.

Biddle, Robert;—B. 8th month 10th, 1844. Married Anna Miller.

> Anna M. Biddle;—B. 8th month 2nd, 1823; M. 12th month 1st, 1842.

Biddle, William Canby;—B. 9th month 25th, 1816. Married
    Rachel Miller.
    Rachel M. Biddle;—B. 10th month 11th, 1818; M. 2nd
        month 21st, 1838.
Biddle, Henry;—B. 1st month 1st, 1818; D. 8th month 31st,
    1818.
Biddle, Clement;—B. 11th month 17th, 1819. Married first,
    Susan T. Walton.
        Susan T. Biddle;—B. 10th month, 1820; M. 9th month 9th,
            1841; D. 12th month 6th, 1842.
    Married second, Susan W. Cadwallader.
        Susan W. Biddle;—B. 3rd month 9th, 1823; M. 4th month
            10th, 1845.
Biddle, Anne;—B. 11th month 18th, 1822.

Anna C. and David Smyth.

Smyth, Lindley;—B. 7th month 28th, 1816. Married Elizabeth
    S. Ferris.
        Elizabeth F. Smyth;—B. 2nd month 6th, 1819; M. 10th
            month 3rd, 1839.
Smyth, Sarah Morris;—B. 7th month 3rd, 1819; D. 6th month
    26th, 1826.

Smyth, Lucy;—B. 9th month 13th, 1820

Smyth, William Canby;—B. 2nd month 11th, 1823. Married
Emily Betts.

    Emily B. Smyth;—B. 1st month 10th, 1823; M. 9th month
28th, 1847.

Smyth, Mary Anna;—B. 8th month 14th, 1824.

Smyth, Clement Biddle;—B. 12th month 29th, 1827. Married
Sarah A. Sellers.

    Sarah S. Smyth;—B. 8th month 22nd, 1828; M. 6th
month 4th, 1856.

Merrit and Eliza T. Canby.

Canby, William Marriott;—B. 3rd month 17th, 1831. Married
Edith Dillon Mathews.

    Edith D. Canby;—B. 10th month 3rd, 1835; M. 6th month
15th, 1870.

Canby, Anna Tatnall;—B. 6th month 29th, 1833.

Canby, Martha, Married Elliston Perot Morris;—B. 5th month
22nd, 1831.

    Martha C. Morris;—B. 5th month 12th, 1836; M. 3rd
month 21st, 1861.

SIXTH GENERATION.

David and Sarah A. Ferris.

Ferris, Francis Canby;—B. 3rd month 22nd, 1850; D. 1st month 15th, 1880.

Ferris, William Canby;—B. 11th month 17th, 1851. .

Ferris, Matilda;—B. 8th month 19th, 1853.

Ferris, Henry;—B. 8th month 16th, 1855.

Ferris, Alfred ;—B. 6th month 21st, 1864.

Ferris, Walter ;—B. 3rd month 21st, 1868.

William and Mary W. Ferris.

Ferris, Fanny. Married Charles Hallowell; B. 12th month
1sth, 1843.

Fanny. F. Hallowell ;—B. 3rd month 20th, 1846; M. 6th
mouth 11th, 1868.

Ferris, Benjamin ;—B. 7th month 24th, 1847. Married Rachel
Richardson.

Rachel R. Ferris ;—B. 9th month 1st, 1845 ; M. 2nd month
25th, 1879.

Ferris, Joseph W. ;—B. 4th month 6th, 1849; D. 1st month
19th, 1858.

Ferris, Mary H., Married Eldridge C. Price ;—B. 2nd month
21st, 1854.

Mary H. Price ;—B 9th month 3rd, 1854 ; M. 10th month
10th, 1877.

Ferris, William, Jr. ;—B. 7th month 26th, 1859.

Ferris, Deborah, Jr. ;—B. 3rd month 27th, 1863.

Ferris, Anna M., Jr. ;—B. 11th month 5th, 1864.

Edward and Catharine L. Ferris.

Ferris, Edith;—B. 9th month 27th, 1856.

Ferris, George A.;—B. 1st month 31st, 1859.

Ferris, Katharine L.;—B. 2nd month 13th, 1865.

Robert and Anna M. Biddle.

Biddle, Charles Miller;—B. 2nd month 3rd, 1844. Married Hannah McIlvain.

    Hannah M. Biddle;—B. 4th month 12th, 1848; M. 11th month 19th, 1868.

Biddle, Henry Canby;—B. 10th month 12th, 1845. Married Anna Mary McIlvain.

    Anna Mary M. Biddle;—B. 9th month 14th, 1850; M. 11th month 2nd, 1876.

Biddle, Hannah Miller, Married John C. W. Frishmuth;—B. 4th month 3rd, 1844.

Hannah B. Frishmuth;—B. 8th month 24th, 1850; M. 1st month 5th, 1882.

Biddle, Elizabeth Parrish;—Married John C. W. Frishmuth, B. 4th month 3rd, 1844.

Elizabeth B. Frishmuth;—B. 8th month 1st, 1853; M. 6th month 3rd, 1875; D. 12th month 17th, 1879.

Biddle, Martha Canby;—B. 12th month 3rd, 1854.

Wm. Canby and Rachel M. Biddle.

Biddle, Clement Miller;—B. 12th month 24th, 1838. Married Lydia Cooper.

Lydia C. Biddle;—B. 1st month 4th, 1841; M. 10th month 11th, 1860.

Biddle, Frances Canby, Married Clement Acton Griscom;—B. 3rd month 15th, 1841.

Frances C. Griscom;—B. 8th month 11th, 1840; M. 6th month 18th, 1862.

Biddle, Helen, Married George Brinton Thomas;—B. 7th month 5th, 1836.

Helen B. Thomas;—B. 3rd month 25th, 1844; M. 9th month 17th, 1866; D. 3rd month 28th, 1877.

Biddle, Mary, Married Howard Wood;—B. 2nd month 8th, 1846.

Mary B. Wood;—B. 12th month 17th, 1849; M. 1st month 28th, 1869.

Biddle, Hannah Nicholson, Married Charles Williams;—B. 11th month 22nd, 1851.

Hannah B. Williams;—B. 4th month 18th, 1855; M. 10th month 18th, 1877.

Clement and Susan T. Biddle.

Biddle, William Walton;—B. 7th month 14th, 1842. Married Mary Taggart.

Màry T. Biddle;—B. 5th month 1st, 1846; M. 4th month 22nd, 1874.

Clement and Susan W. Biddle.

Biddle, Canby;—B. 2nd month 23rd, 1846; D. 4th month 13th. 1857.

Biddle, Francis Cadwallader;—B. 9th month 16th, 1851.
Married Sarah Pennock.

Sarah P. Biddle;—B. 2nd month 3rd, 1849; M. 10th month
22nd, 1873.

Biddle, Anne;—B. 3rd month 2nd, 1857.

Lindley and Elizabeth F. Smyth.

Smyth, Ferris;—B. 9th month 8th, 1841; D. 4th month 2nd,
1843.

Smyth, Horace;—B. 3rd month 9th, 1844. Married Mary E.
Hanson.

Mary H. Smyth;—B. 1st month 2nd, 1842; M. 10th
month 3rd, 1865.

Smyth, Marriott Canby;—B. 11th month 13th, 1845. Married
Clara Lauderback.

Clara L. Smyth :—B. 9th month 28th, 1848 ; M. 11th month
14th, 1875.

William C. and Emily B. Smyth.

Smyth, Mary Betts :—B. 6th month 23rd, 1848 ; D. 8th month
10th, 1872.

Smyth, Anna Canby ;—Married Nathaniel E. Janney, B. 3rd
month 5th, 1842.

Anna C. Janney :—B. 3rd month 23rd, 1850 ; M. 10th
month 16th, 1877.

Smyth, Lindley ;—B. 8th month 12th, 1852 ; D. 2nd month
17th, 1853.

Smyth, Lucy ;—Married Howard M. Cooper, B. 6th month
24th, 1844.

Lucy S. Cooper ;—B. 11th month 28th, 1853 ; M. 4th
month 22nd, 1884.

Smyth, Emily Betts ;—B. 12th month 4th, 1855.

Smyth, Frances Canby ;—B 10th month 22nd, 1858.

Smyth, Edward Betts ;—B. 10th month 22nd, 1869.

Clement B. and Sarah S. Smyth.

Smyth, Herbert Weir ;—B. 8th month 28th, 1857.

Smyth, Elizabeth Sellers ;—B. 8th month 4th, 1860; D. 10th month 29th, 1861.

Smyth, William Canby ;—B. 12th month 28th, 1864; D. 7th mouth 28th, 1875.

Smyth, Alice Pearson ;—B. 8th month 28th, 1866.

William M. and Edith D. Canby.

Canby, Marriott ;—B. 4th month 7th, 1871.

Canby, Henry Mathews ;—B. 6th month 17th, 1874.

Canby, William Shipley ;—B. 12th month 24th, 1875 ; D. 12th month 10th, 1882.

Martha C. and Elliston P. Morris.

Morris, Marriott Canby ;—B. 9th month 7th, 1863.

Morris, Elizabeth Canby ;—B. 10th month 4th, 1866.

Morris, Samuel Buckley;—B. 10th month 10th, 1868.

Morris, E. Perot;—B. 5th month 31st, 1872; D. 3rd month 10th, 1881.

SEVENTH GENERATION.

Fanny F. and Charles Hallowell.

Hallowell, Wm. Ferris;—B. 5th month 30th, 1869.

Hallowell, Charles S. ;—B. 1st month 31st, 1872.

Hallowell, Benjamin S. ;—B. 12th month 18th, 1873; D. 12th
   month 26th, 1874.

Hallowell, Lewis B. ;—B. 4th month 11th, 1877.

Mary H. and Eldridge C. Price.

Price, Marriott ;—B. 6th month 7th, 1881.

Charles M. and Hannah M. Biddle.

Biddle, Anna ;—B. 11th month 24th, 1869.

Biddle, Martha McIlvain ;—B. 3rd month 28th, 1871.

Biddle, Helen ;—B. 5th month 16th, 1875.

Biddle, Hannah M.,

Biddle, Charles M., } B. 8th month 14th, 1878.

Biddle, Robert, Jr. ;—B. 2nd month 19th, 1880.

Henry C. and Anna Mary M. Biddle.

Biddle, Hugh McIlvain ;—B. 8th month 29th, 1877.

Biddle, Mary ;—B. 3rd month 19th, 1879.

Biddle, Henry C., Jr. ;—B. 4th month 11th, 1880.

Biddle, Lilian ;—B. 7th month 11th, 1881.

Elizabeth B. and John C. W. Frishmuth.

Frishmuth, Anna Biddle,

} B. 2nd month 22nd, 1876.

Frishmuth, Mary Grandom,

Hannah B. and John C. W. Frishmuth.

Frishmuth, Edna Helen ;—B. 8th month 16th, 1883.

Clement M. and Lydia C. Biddle.

Biddle, Lucy ;—Married J. Reece Lewis; B. 4th month 13th, 1856.

Lucy Biddle Lewis ;—B. 9th month 26th, 1861; M. 9th month 25th, 1884.

Biddle, Wm. Canby, Jr. ;—B. 6th month 2nd, 1864.

Biddle, Robert, Jr. ;—B. 5th month 31st, 1867.

Biddle, Caroline Cooper ;—B. 3rd month 13th, 1871.

Biddle, Lydia ;—B. 9th month 13th, 1873.

Biddle, Clement Miller, Jr. ;—B. 8th month 22nd, 1876.

Frances C. and Clement A. Griscom.

Griscom, John Acton ;—B. 3rd month 31st, 1863; D. 7th
    month 15th, 1864.

Griscom, Helen Biddle ;—B. 10th month 9th, 1866.

Griscom, Clement Acton ;—B. 6th month 20th, 1868.

Griscom, Rodman Ellison ;—B. 10th month 21st, 1870.

Griscom, Lloyd Carpenter ;—B. 11th month 4th, 1872.

Griscom, Frances Canby ;—B. 4th month 19th, 1879.

Helen B. and George B. Thomas.

Thomas, Frances Canby ;—B. 7th month 2nd, 1867.

Thomas, Isaac Biddle ;—B. 6th month 26th, 1872.

Thomas, Rachel Miller ;—B. 4th month 21st, 1875.

Mary B. and Howard Wood.

Wood, Biddle ;—B. 12th month 22nd, 1869.

Wood, Helen Biddle;—B. 12th month 22nd, 1872.

Wood, Alan ;—B. 3rd month 1st, 1874.

Wood, Howard ;—B. 9th month 20th, 1876.

Wood, Clement Biddle ;—B. 7th month 13th, 1878.

Wood, Owen Biddle;—B. 3rd month 4th, 1880; D. 2nd month 26th, 1882.
Wood, Rachel Biddle;—B. 1st month 29th, 1882.

Wood, Marion Biddle;—B. 8th month 13th, 1884.

Hannah B. and Charles Williams.

Williams, William Biddle ;—B. 10th month 7th, 1878.

Williams, Frances Biddle ;—B. 2nd month 17th, 1884.

William W. and Mary T. Biddle.

Biddle, Edward Taggart ;—B. 4th month 9th, 1875.

Biddle, William Canby ;—B. 9th month 11th, 1877.

Biddle, Ferris ;—B. 7th month 31st, 1879 ; D. 5th month 7th, 1880.

Biddle, Howard ;—B. 2nd month 10th, 1882.

Francis C. and Sarah P. Biddle.

Biddle, Lydia Pennock ;—B. 9th month 16th, 1874.

Horace and Mary H. Smyth.

Smyth, Elizabeth Ferris ;—B. 7th month 9th, 1866.
Smyth, Percival Hanson ;—B. 2nd month 12th, 1868.

Marriott and Clara L. Smyth.

Smyth, Frances ;—B. 12th month 22nd, 1878.
Smyth, Marion ;—B. 7th month 9th, 1880.

Smyth, Lindley ;—B. 3rd month 6th, 1882.

Anna Canby and Nathaniel E. Janney.

Janney, Wm. Canby ;—B. 3rd month 7th, 1880.
Janney, Emily ;—B. 6th month 17th 1882.

www.ingramcontent.com/pod-product-compliance
Lightning Source LLC
Chambersburg PA
CBHW021640270326
41931CB00008B/1099